: POETRY FORUM :
10.
04

POETRY FORUM : A PLAY POEM : A PL'EM
Copyright © 2006 by Judith Hall and David Lehman

Published by: Bayeux Arts, Inc., 119 Stratton Crescent SW,
Calgary, Canada T3H 1T7, www.bayeux.com

Poetry Forum was performed at the New School in October 2004.

"Act Two, Scene Three" (as "The Old Constellation")
originally appeared in *The Antioch Review.*

The authors wish to thank Alec Bernstein, Molly Bernstein,
Tracy Shapiro, and F.D. Reeve for critical support.

Library and Archives Canada Cataloguing in Publication

Hall, Judith, 1951-
     Poetry forum : a play poem : a pl'em / Judith Hall,
     David Lehman.

ISBN 1-896209-79-3

     I. Lehman, David, 1948- II. Title.
PS3558.A3695P63 2006   812'.54   C2006-905379-0

First Printing: April 2007
Printed in Canada

*Books published by Bayeux Arts/Gondolier are available at special quantity
discounts to use as premiums and sales promotions, or for use in corpo-
rate training programs. For more information, please write to Special Sales,
Bayeux Arts, Inc., 119 Stratton Crescent SW, Calgary, Canada T3H 1T7.*

The publishing activities of Bayeux/Gondolier are supported by the Canada
Council for the Arts, the Alberta Foundation for the Arts, and by the Govern-
ment of Canada through its Book Publishing Industry Development Program.

POETRY FORUM : A PLAY POEM : A PL'EM
by
JUDITH HALL and DAVID LEHMAN

ACT ONE

FOR YEARS I WAS SMART. I RECOMMEND PLEASANT.

CHASE , HARVEY

SCENE : BEFORE THE FORUM

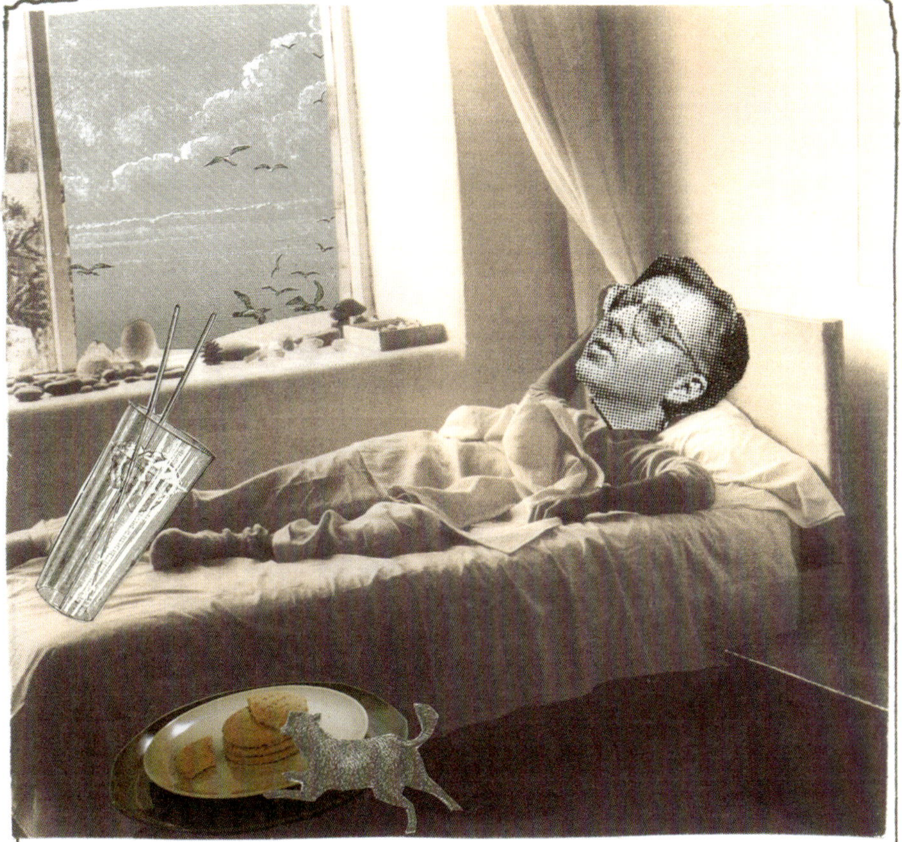

David: I write every day.

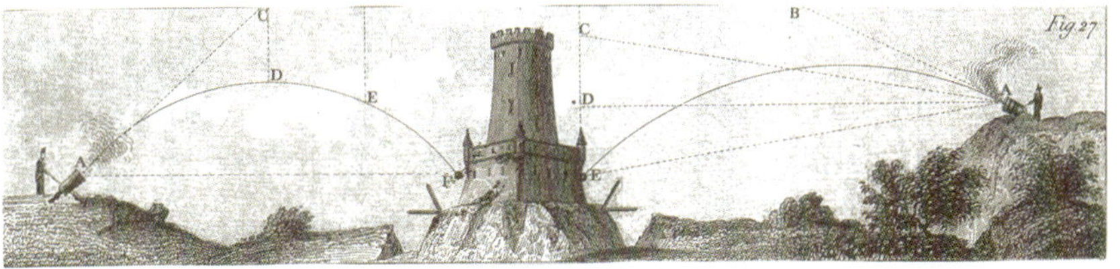

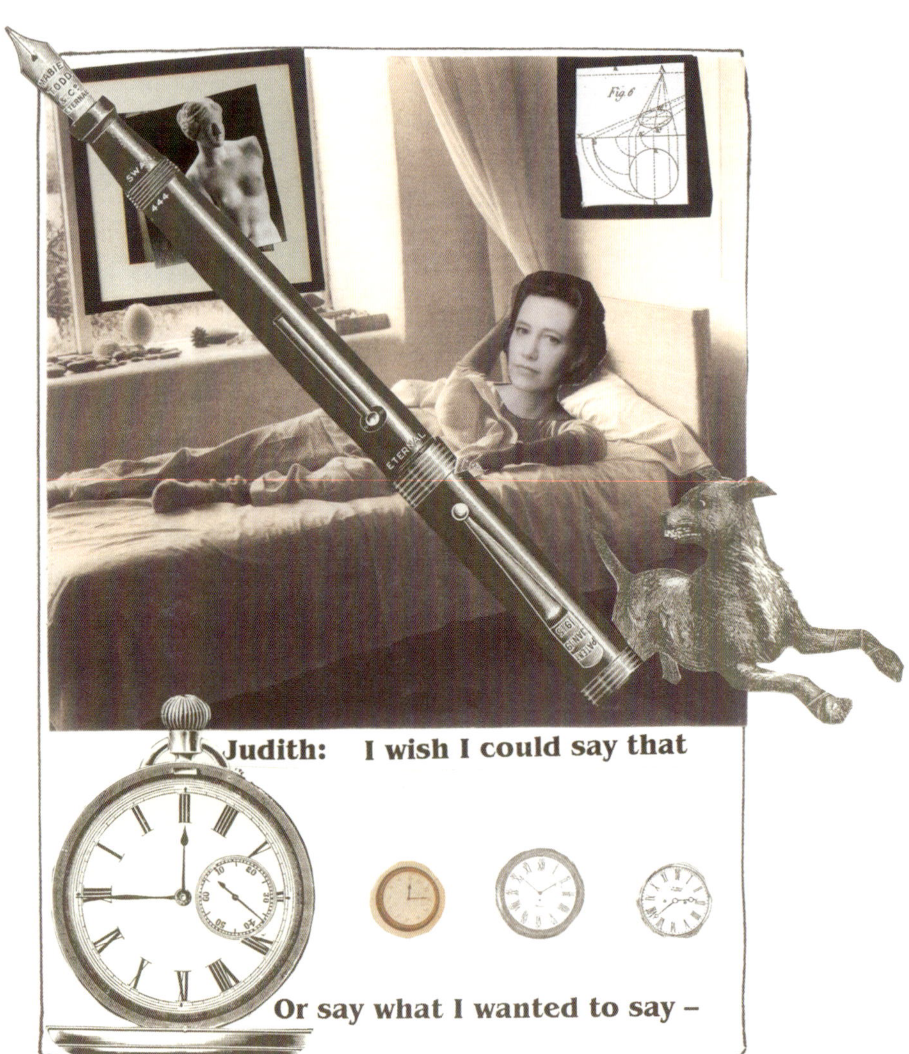

Judith: I wish I could say that

Or say what I wanted to say –

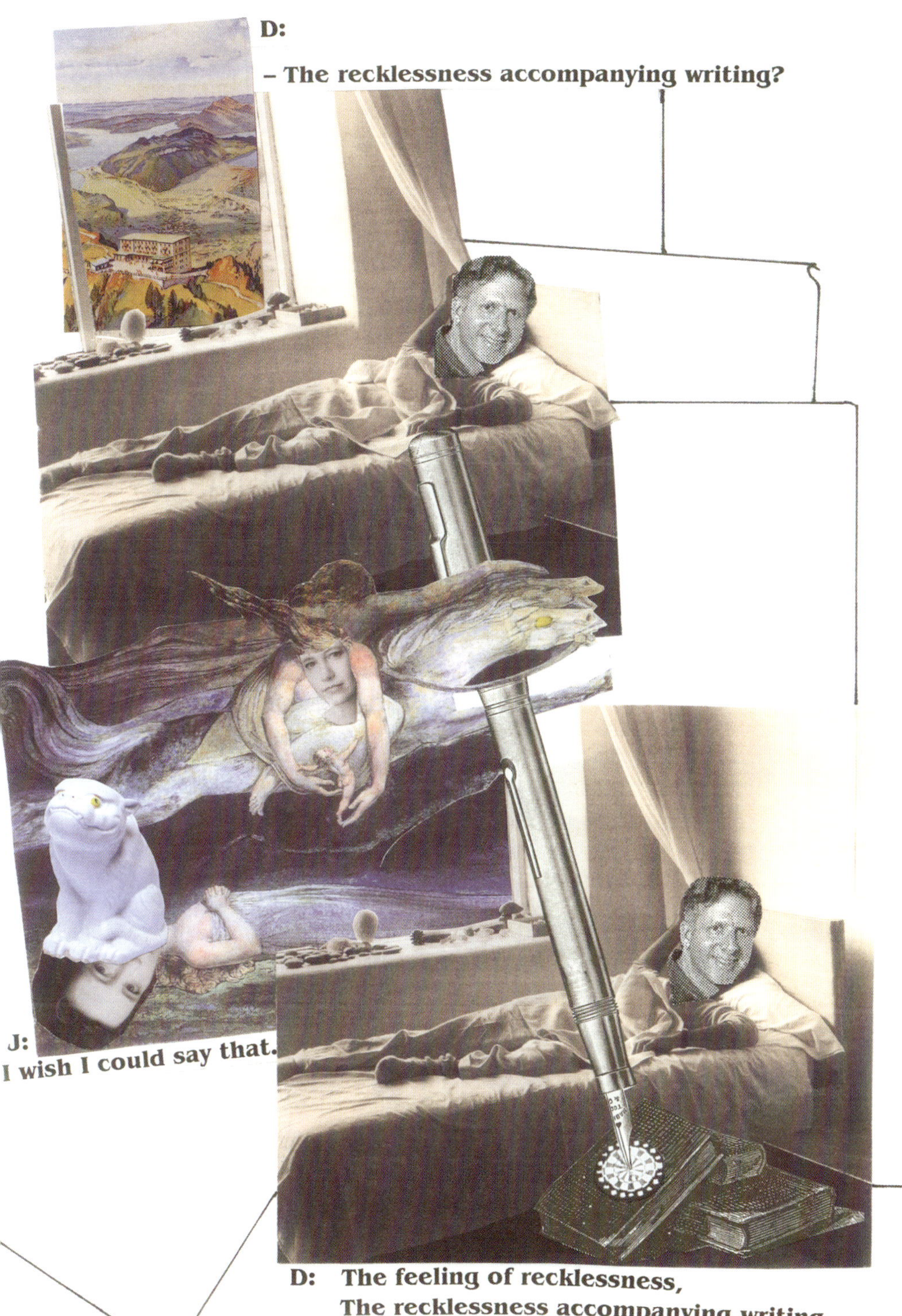

D:
– The recklessness accompanying writing?
J:
I wish I could say that.
D: The feeling of recklessness,
      The recklessness accompanying writing –

J:
Unencumbered by prepositions . . .

D:
The feeling of recklessness –

J: Not writing "for" or writing "to," "on,"
Unencumbered by prepositions.

D: **Not more**

abstract, mediated expression!

J:

Not writing "for" or writing "to," "on" . . .

D:

Then you do not write for friends
But more abstract, mediated expression!

Under under under under under
Under
Under
UNDER UNDER
NDER U
under
under
under
under
under
under
Under the table
UNDER U
UNDER U
UNDER U
UNDER U
UNDER U
UNDER U
UNDER U
UNDER U
UNDER U
J:
I demonstrated prepositions on
TV.
I'M
UNDER
ARE YOU

D: Then you do not write for friends.

J: Or "under" or "over" or "after" them,
                        Like demonstrating prepositions on TV.

D: Together,

we nearly sound like James Dean.

<table>
<tr><td>J:</td><td>"Under" or "over" our Causes? Or "after" them?</td></tr>
<tr><td>D:</td><td>Beyond the baggage of "confused youth."
Together we nearly sound like James Dean.</td></tr>
</table>

J: For years I was confused. "I recommend   pleasant."

D: Beyond the baggage of "confused youth."

J: Oh, say what I wanted to say!
        For years I was confused. "I recommend pleasant."

D: I write every day.

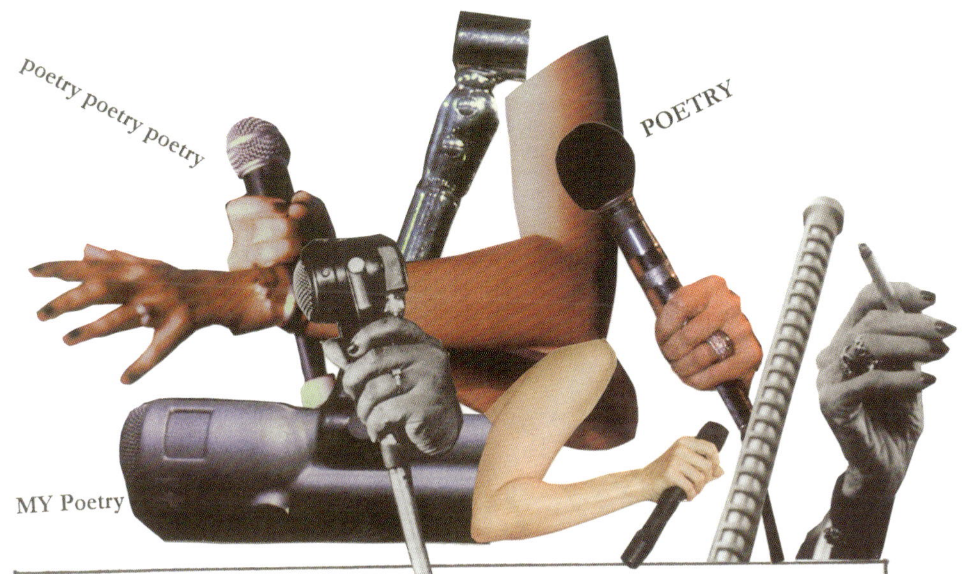

ACT TWO

INSTINCTIVELY, HE HAD ALREADY TRAINED HIMSELF IN THE HABIT OF PRETENDING HE WAS SOMEONE, SO IT SHOULD NOT BE DISCOVERED THAT HE WAS NO ONE.

BORGES (tr., KERRIGAN), "EVERYTHING and NOTHING"

SCENE : AT THE PODIUM

Hall:

(And here I'm made to say something pompous
And obvious) ABOUT POETRY:

Let it instruct and sing and so on. Delight.

Although we don't hear much about instruction
After years of insistent delight.
Romantic, then "avant-garde" delight:
Doctrinal . . . commodified delights . . .

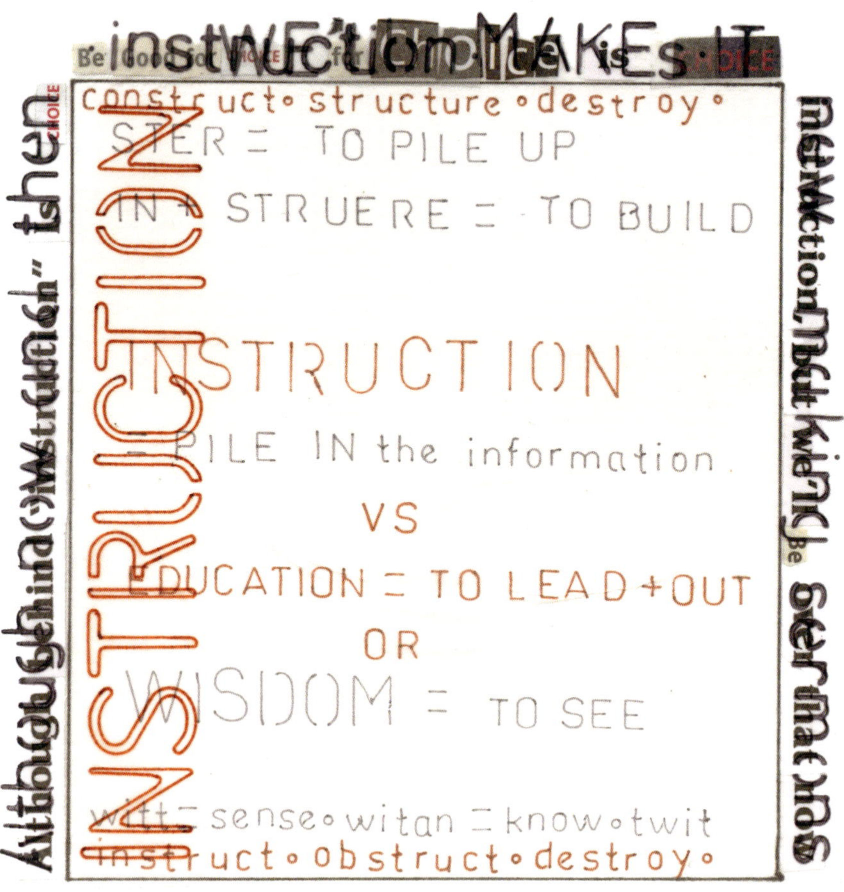

Although now that our post-modernism
Is over, is "instruction" far behind?
Not simple-minded consolation but instruction,
   "Wisdom": Dame Reason? Damn wit?
    . . . And then we'll *make it new* making sermons?

The Man in the Back Row:

> But is it not provincial – sentimental –
> The idea of "making it new," your American fetish
> Of novelty, American novelties,
> Disposable American poems –
> In the context of a global economy?

Hall: Are we sentimental about disposable poems?
Yes. Is it American? Human?
Making it new made sense mid-century,
Just as the pastiche made sense in the end,
Economically, then aesthetically.

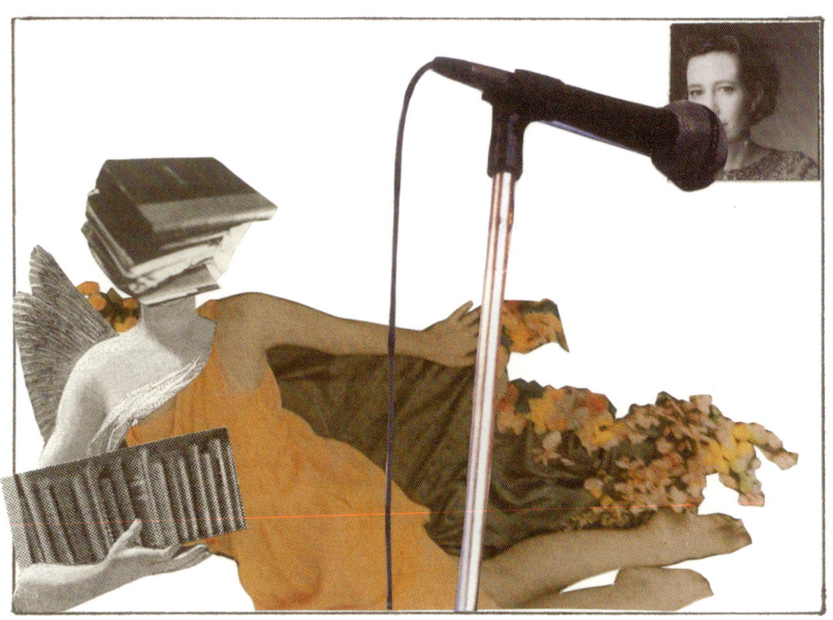

The Man: And now?
Hall: Now?
The Man: Now "accessibility"
          Is not the next best thing to heaven.

Hall: Nor is "obscurity".
The Man: Nor fame –
Hall: Nor sales (*sigh*).

If I criss-cross the country thinking *sales*,
Let me do it in one of those belabored
Experimental spectacles of *Death* –
Not dreaming of poetry in a global economy
And whether or not my slim volumes sell –

But *me* – the edifying Willy Loman,
The wife singing RESPECT WILL BE PAID,
For the effort on behalf of language
And poets (talk about a thankless job) who

RESPECT the intellection – of intuition –
And ask more of THE POEM than escape.

SCENE : IN THE POWDER ROOM

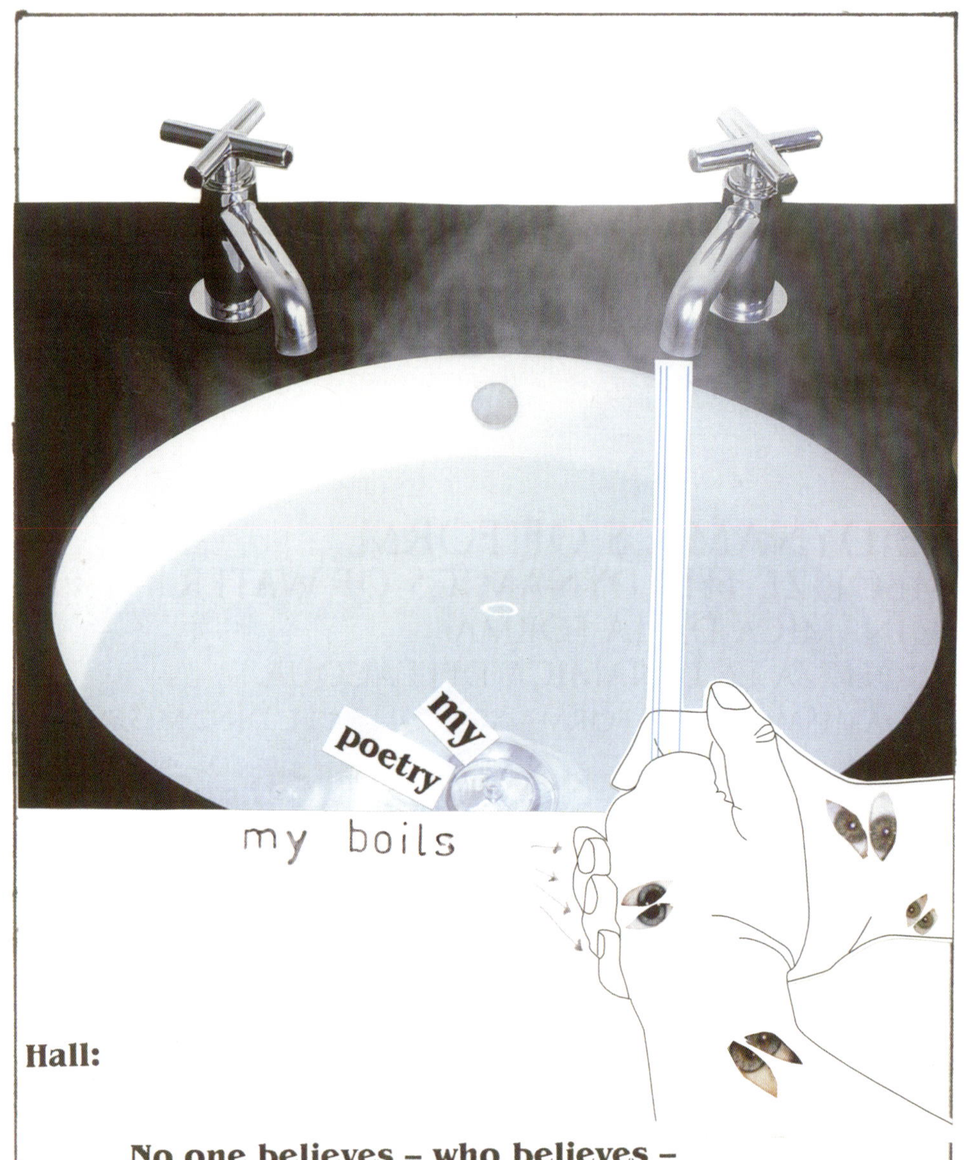

Hall:

No one believes – who believes –
POETRY   could be a "job"?

"THE POET,"   brooding "Job" :

Boo-hoo,

my "full-throated ease" commodified to PLEASE?

These dramas, public moments, sap, sapping; a sap,

c'est moi!   (AARGH!)

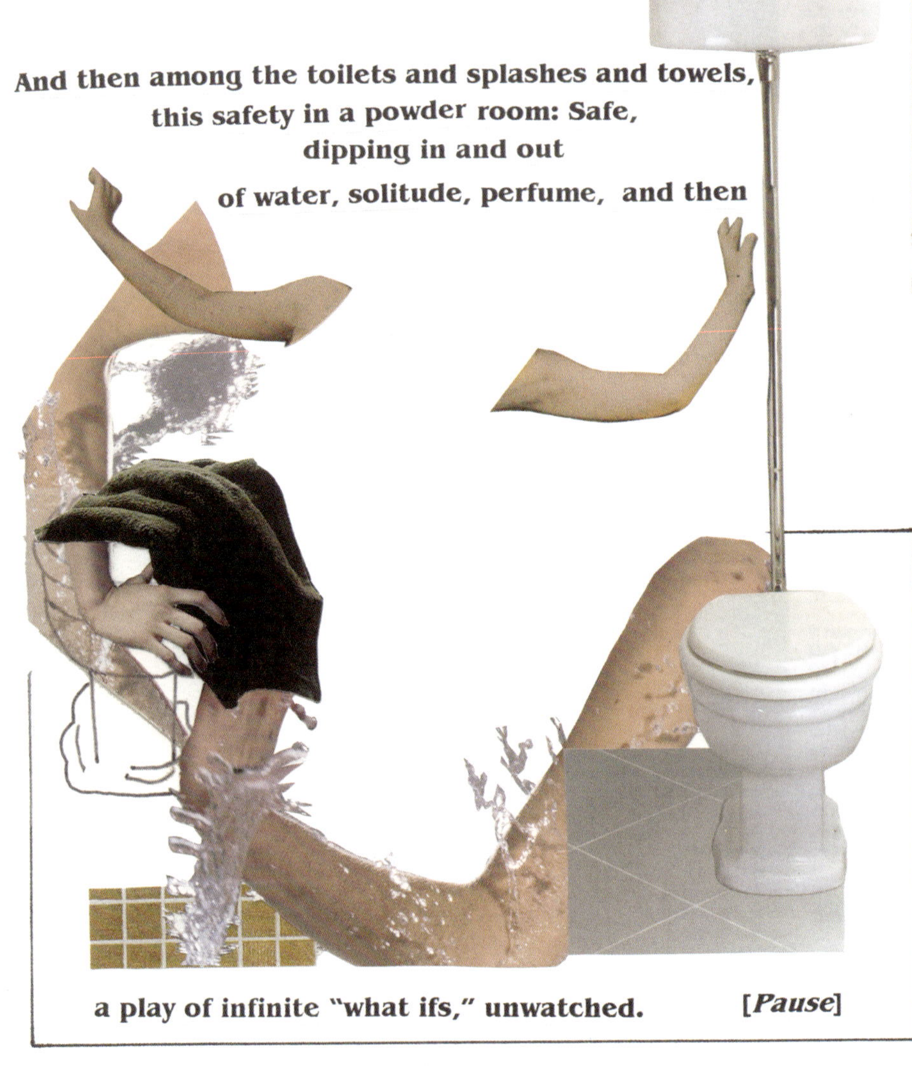

And then among the toilets and splashes and towels,
this safety in a powder room: Safe,
dipping in and out
of water, solitude, perfume, and then

a play of infinite "what ifs," unwatched.   [*Pause*]

No armor in the powder room; no answers; no

answers as   armor;

sitting for a minute in the lounge; no mirrors;

nothing and nothing said.

Because only then is the poem possible,

if "THE POET" IS IMPOSSIBLE?

If the scene erases, annihilates,

like a posse making the hero safe?

"The Old Constellation"

The old constellation of wish, word, guilt, pleasure, shame.

– Hall

SCENE : OUTSIDE THE POWDER ROOM

Other people go to bed. I just sit and wish
for nothing much, just to know the word
when I hear it and not to feel the guilt
that other people associate with pleasure,
or something more primal than guilt, shame,
which is what you get for having a body.

What can be worse than not having a body?
(In my veins there is a wish.)
Money is to shit as guilt is to shame
as the sentence is to the word.
Is that understood? It's been a pleasure
to serve you, said the Commissioner of Guilt.

wish

Some soldiers can kill without feeling guilt.
I learned I wasn't one of them. I was anybody
in a uniform, and staying alive wasn't a pleasure
but a duty. Some of the injured wished
they had died, a wish seldom put into words
without feelings of shame.

If the women we loved were unashamed,
it was because they obeyed the laws of guilt
and loved the men who wooed them with words
in praise of their yielding bodies.
I asked her, did she get her wish?
She said yes but it gave her no pleasure.

The poem's first purpose is to give pleasure
and defeat the formidable forces of shame
that would twist every healthy lusty wish
into a dark confession of guilt
and a renunciation of the body:
the word without flesh, the naked, shivering word.

I who believe in the constellations of the word
would construct a planetarium of pleasure
for my friends, where each heavenly body
can be contemplated without the shame
of a pretty librarian or the guilt
of a veteran who pulled the trigger of a wish.

The word is the result of the wish for the word.
Not every pleasure is a guilty one.
A shame it would be to forsake love's body.

SCENE : NEAR THE HALL

David: I thought we lost you in the ladies' room.
Judith: I thought I'd exemplify solitude
          (The benefits of nothingness) for students –

D: Not the *cost* of nothingness – [*he fumes*]

Now we're late – hear them all leave – while you

Decide lolly-gagging in the ladies' room
Is "existential," "potentially" illuminating –
Some triumphant *Ariel*-without-the-gas coup –

J: No. Poetry – lyric poetry – isn't social.

And the body – seen – socializes song,
Unless it's altered, masked, abject, outre.

I am not what you hear on the page.

And audiences, looking at the poet
As they listen, intermittently,

Forget about the page, the poor dear page.
They receive, for the first time, the poem
As tepid spectacle, "performance," the "brave"
Part of another cult of personality,

Seeing the poem leave the poet's body.

D: **What if I AM what you hear?**

J: **The lamb? That invention**

                                         That leaps and overleaps identity?

D: "Identity?" Some prefer chaos; others, stars.

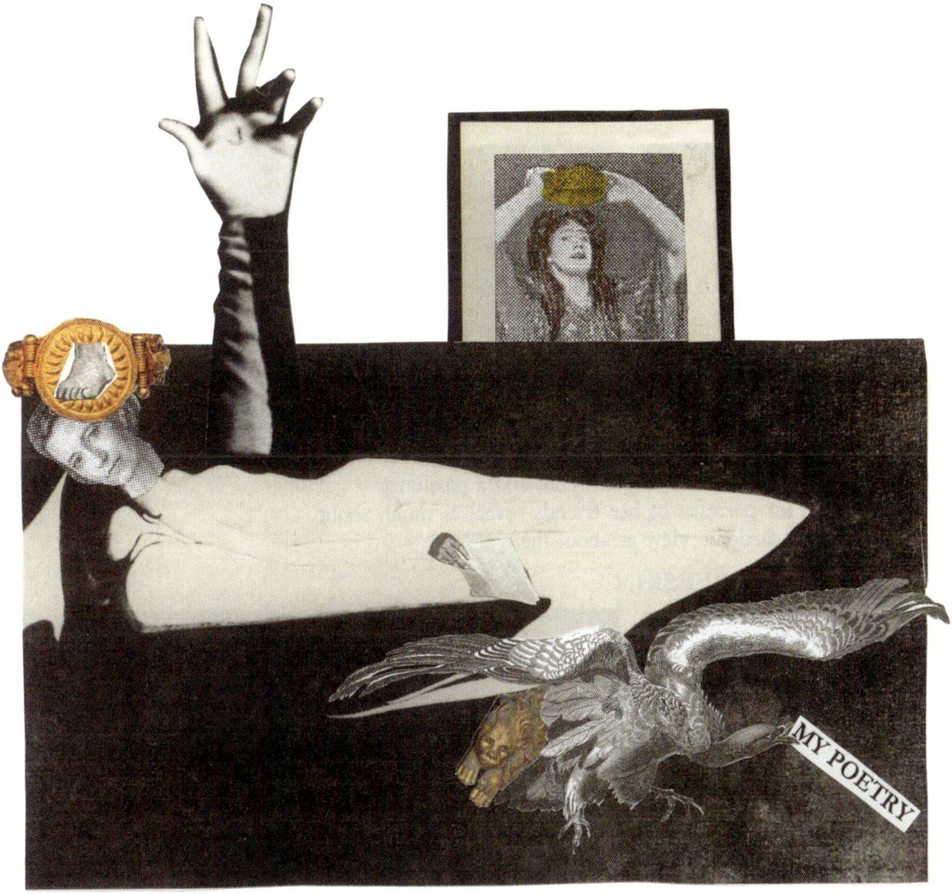

J:

'Tis safer to be that which we destroy
Than by destruction dwell in doubtful joy.

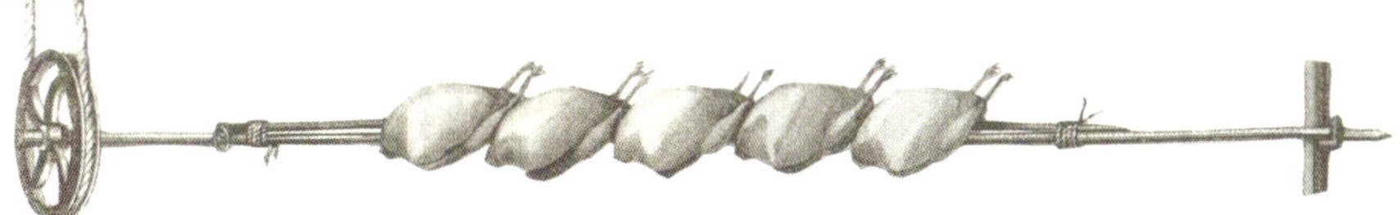

ACT THREE

SCENE : AFTER THE FORUM

David:

To write or to be blocked – to write or not:
That is the answer, but what is the question?

When the world's more frayed than a pair of pants
Worn by a beggar disguised as a man
Who fought in the Trojan War and has returned
To his faithless wife, who wants to know
Whether his pen and his penis are one or is

The idea that gender is a dimension of art

Hooey? I know I need to write this down:

To smoke or not to smoke when writing is
The question that set off the fire alarm,
But think of all the other questions no one
Had the wit or the pluck to ask the speaker.

To love or to be loved; if that's the choice –
To die before or after your mate; to live

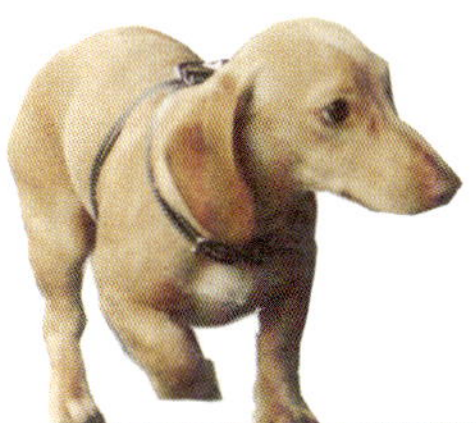

In the mind that lives in the past and drinks too much;

To be happy or to be Holderlin, if that's
The choice, as it can never be in life;

To love to write yet feel the sanctity of silence –

That's as fake a line as I've written
Since Christopher Ricks rewrote the last line
Of Tennyson's "Ulysses," which is
"To strive, to seek, to find, and not to yield";

Ricks hears, but he's a critic. Not to yield

  The right of way to a dumb-ass when driving
  A car in a strange country of the blind
  Where the blind alone are allowed to drive
  Is my policy, and I know who I am,

A player in a play by someone else,
Who goes to the bar with the rest of the cast
After the show is over, and has a beer,

And walks home alone: and no one looking
Can tell that this poor player's a poet.

THE CAST

Akhmatova, Anna
Arendt, Hannah
Ashbery, John
Auden, W. H.
Bacall, Lauren
Bergman, Ingrid
Berryman, John
Blake, William
Bogan, Louise
Bogart, Humphrey
Brooks, Gwendolyn
Callas, Maria
Colette
Creature from the Black Lagoon
Dean, James
Dickinson, Emily
Dietrich, Marlene
Einstein, Albert
Eliot, T.S.
Fields, W.C.
Forti, Simone
Frost, Robert
Garland, Judy
Ginsberg, Allen
Grant, Cary
Hall, Judith
Hayworth, Rita
Hepburn, Katharine
Holderlin, Friedrich
Homer
Hopkins, Gerard Manley
Hughes, Langston
Jones, Leroi (Amiri Baraka)
Joyce, James

Keats, John
Lehman, David
Lowell, Robert
Millay, Edna St. Vincent
Milton, John
Moore, Marianne
Nadelman, Elie
Neruda, Pablo
O'Hara, Frank
Ovid
Pasternak, Boris
Plath, Sylvia
Poe, Edgar Allan
Pound, Ezra
Proust, Marcel
Roethke, Theodore
Sandburg, Carl
Sargent, John Singer
Sappho
Sartre, Jean Paul
Shakespeare, William
Sinatra, Frank
Smith, Stevie
Stein, Gertrude
Stevens, Wallace
Tennyson, Alfred, Lord
Terry, Ellen
Thomas, Dylan
Warhol, Andy
Wayne, John
West, Mae
Whitman, Walt
Woolf, Virginia
Yeats, William Butler

THE AUTHORS

JUDITH HALL is the author of four collections of poetry, including *Three Trios* (2006). She has received awards from the Guggenheim Foundation, the Ingram Merrill Foundation, and the National Endowment for the Arts. She serves as poetry editor of *The Antioch Review* and teaches at California Institute of Technology and with the graduate writing program at New England College.

DAVID LEHMAN is the author of six collections of poetry, most recently *When a Woman Loves a Man* (2005). His non-fiction works include *The Last Avant-Garde: The Making of the New York School of Poets* (1998) and *Signs of the Times: Deconstruction and the Fall of Paul de Man* (1991). He teaches writing and literature in the graduate writing program at the New School. In 1988, he launched the Best American Poetry anthology series.

POETRY FORUM : A PL'EM
THE
END